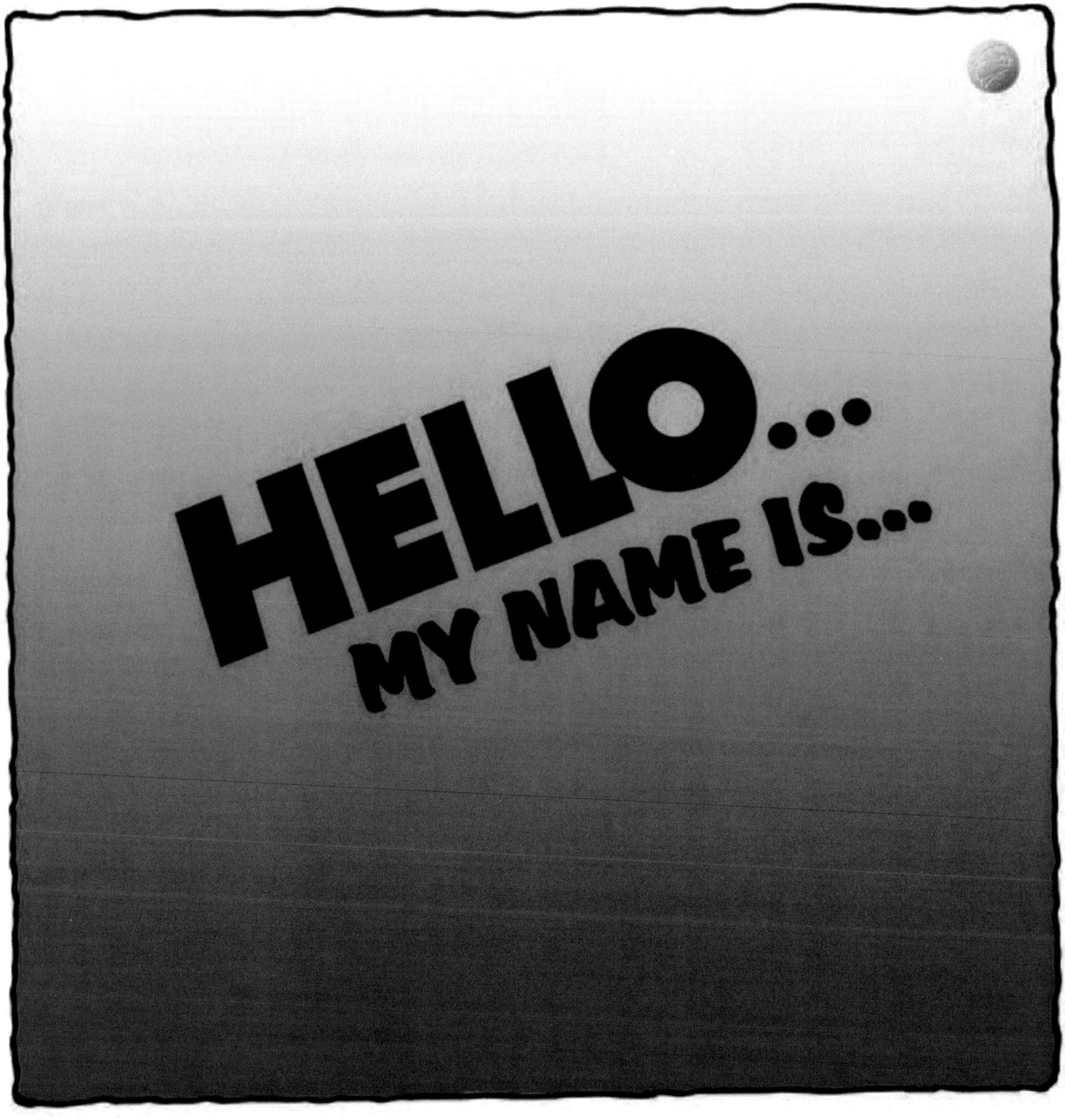
HELLO...
MY NAME IS...

AuthorHouse™
1663 Liberty Drive
Bloomington, IN 47403
www.authorhouse.com
Phone: 1 (800) 839-8640

Published by AuthorHouse 01/14/2015

ISBN: 978-1-4969-6456-4 (sc)
ISBN: 978-1-4969-6457-1 (e)

Library of Congress Control Number: 2015900619

Any people depicted in stock imagery provided by Thinkstock are models,
and such images are being used for illustrative purposes only.

This book is printed on acid-free paper.

authorHOUSE®

INTRODUCTION:

I have been collecting interesting names for about 35 years. Each day I would check the obituaries to see if any of the flock in my church had left us. I came to realize that parents had given kids interesting and sometimes cruel names to carry through life. Names have great power. They create an image and you wonder what people look like.This book will help you with some of the names.

Many have made the best of a bad name and succeeded in life; others did not. I saw a news article that a David Urah Payne was charged with murder. Ima Hogg became a famous Houston socialite and now has a museum in her honor.The Bible tells us that names are important and some day we will get a new name from God. This will really be a great day for some of us!

Well, God saw me collecting these names and showed me He has a real sense of humor. My neighbor wanted me to do his wedding. His name was Leonard Crapoff Jr. That went well as you do not need to say the last name until the end of the wedding. Later, his father died and he asked me to do the funeral. Now I had to begin the service by saying, "We are gathered in loving memory of Leonard P. Crapoff." Then I had to keep a straight face for the rest of the service.

This book contains no sexual innuendos; but bodily functions are fair game.

The King family heads my list of great names. Joe King makes many smile. Mel King would be a great name for a farmer. Lee King would not make a good ship captain. I found a funeral home in Buffalo named Amigone. Would you go to a surgeon named Butcher? Oh, I almost forgot Ella Fant of Galesburg. Really!!

If you find names for my next edition, or would like more copies, email me at chsh527@oceana.net

Enjoy!

Chuck Anderson

HELLO...
MY NAME IS...

JOE KING

VI KING

MEL KING

LEE KING

PATTI K. KING

ADA KLOK

NINA KLOK

EVELYN A. KLOK

SUGAR CANE

NOVA CANE

CANDY CANE

CLIFF HANGER

14

CONSTANCE NORING

NOAH ZARK

NITA BATH

KATZ MEOW

FINKSTROM

SHANDA LEAR

PHY ED CLASS

FINKSTROM

JIM SHORTS

IMA HOGG

DAN DRUFF

OPHELIA LEGG

KERRY OKI

ANITA DOLLAR

MARY LOUISE PANTZEROFF

NAMES AND OCCUPATIONS

Some people have a name that is a perfect match for their job or occupation. Trust us, folks, we didn't make up these incredibly coincidental combinations of funny names of real people and their well-matched careers. All of these combinations are funny, and you'll be amazed at the number of medical professionals whose names perfectly fit their field of expertise.

THOMAS CRAPPER
INVENTOR OF THE FLUSHING TOILET

DOCTOR MOHLER

29

MRS. JIM SCHUH

PHYSICAL EDUCATION TEACHER

PETER POPOFF

TELEVISION EVANGELIST

MRS. SCREECH
VOCAL INSTRUCTOR

DOCTOR KNAPPER

DOCTOR TOOTHACRE

MAJOR MINOR
U.S. MILITARY OFFICER

CHARLES DIGGS
MORTICIAN

DOCTOR BENDER

DOCTORS KATZ & BARKER

DOCTOR BENDOVER
PROCTOLOGIST

C. SHARP MINOR
THEATER ORGANIST

PLUMMER & LEEK
PROFESSIONAL PLUMBERS

RALPH BIBLE

CLERGYMAN

DOCTOR E. Z. FILLER

CHRIS ROACH
EXTERMINATOR

LAWLESS & LYNCH
ATTORNEYS AT LAW

CARDINAL SIN
ARCHBISHOP OF MANILA

I NOW PRONOUNCE YOU...

Love is a wonderful thing...
it often leads to marriage which creates some of the funniest name combinations we have ever seen. It had to be true love when Jodi Pass agreed to marry Bill Gass to become Jodi Pass-Gass! Stan Bye knew when he proposed to his sweetheart, Betty, that she was soon to become Betty Bye. Of course, poor Jack Haase never tied the knot, because no one wanted to marry a Jack Haase!

We also love the wedding announcements in the newspaper. You'll have to agree, the combinations of these names are downright funny!

THE HARDY-HARR WEDDING

OLIVE BRANCH

MARY CHRIS SMITH

LOONEY-WARDE WEDDING

51

JODI PASS-GASS

BETTY BYE

Here are some additional names of real people just to give you a good laugh!

Anita Mann
Barry D. Hachett
Carl Breakdown
Ella Fant
Francis Useless
Hank E. Pankie
Ida Zervbetter
Jan U. Wharry
Kay O'Pectate
Lorraine Inspain
Marsha Mellow
Owen Money
Paul Bearer
Quint S. Henschel

Randy Udderway
Sam Which
Tess Tickle
U. Arnold Phartt
Victor E. Lane
Wayne Dwopp
Xavier Breath
Zack Lee Wright
Desiree Ficker
Canaan Banana
Bea Sting
Bjorn Free
Freida Livery

MAY THEY REST IN PEACE

As we mentioned in the Introduction to this book, many of these funny names of real people were discovered by reading the daily obituaries. We know these people were loved by their families and friends, but, we also know that even the sound of their names will forever put a smile on all of our faces.

Here are a few of our favorite funny names straight from the obituary pages of our local newspapers.

May they rest in peace.

Area Deaths -
David C. Butts
Louise J. Clapper
Reverend U.B. Godman
Clifford C. Hanger

Obituaries:
John P. Daily
Mattie Pothoof
Joyce R. Stiff
Isabell B. Hollerbach

Obituaries:
Dewey B. Hinds
Mary End
Harold Outhouse
Pancras Spitters

Deaths ~
Jerry Attrick
Rufus Leaking
Jack Cass

Obituaries:
Page Turner, Putnam County
Tiny Little, Chatooga County
Joy Rider, Morrow County, Ohio
Frost Snow, Pulaski Co., VA

POSTLUDE

I keep hearing names that would start a new book. Here are a few thoughts that will be free for now.

I mentioned that there was a manure family in Michigan, but I didn't want to touch that. I thought that Henry named his daughter Alota. I dug a little deeper and talked to my brother who said, "I went to school with them. Her name was Alota Johnson. She married Henry and became Alota Manure."

Then there was Allotta Brown who married Rev. Howard Crapp. I hope she did'nt hyphenate her name. Can you imagine introducing her to his church?? "Here is my lovely wife Allota Crapp." (No kidding) I did a wedding for Leonard Crapoff. Maybe Howard was related and dropped the 'off"? He should have dropped the crapp. (Remember Thomas Crapper, the inventor of the flush toilet? Think what he started.)

Now I hear there is a Didee family. Daddy Didee is Bobby Didee. Mamma Didee is Betty Didee. If they had a little one, she could be an itty bitty Didee. What if their daughter grew up and married Howie Dye (son of Harry Dye)? She could be Dodo Didee-Dye (daughter of Betty Didee). What if they bought a funeral home? It would be the Didee Dye mortuary. Then they could buy the Amigone funeral home in Buffalo. That would make the Didee Dye-Amigone Funeral Home. Do not even think about getting the Dokey family from Kalamazoo in that mix. One was O.K. Dokey.

I cannot end this book without a nod to my Swedish heritage. There was a musician in Sweden named Olga Tarstring. She played an unusual instrument. It is called a latrineaccord. It is made by using a new toilet seat. The strings are stretched across the hole. You put the lid behind your head and pluck it. It is, of course, very unusual. People would drive for miles to see this and hear her play. This instrument became so popular; she decided to mass produce it. She tried to get financing from her aunt Hulda Buckback. Hulda lived up to her name and did not support her, so the invention died and is seldom seen even to this day. Hulda, by the way, invested instead in the Nickel Plate railroad. It also went nowhere.

Finally, let's end with a strong word about names. In history a change of name indicated a real change in destiny. Abraham got his new name from God and went on to be the father of two great nations. Paul got his new name and was a champion of the growing church. He stopped killing Christians and was willing to die for being a Christian.

There is a great promise in the Bible that must be encouraging for all. It is especially good for those who have endured difficult names in their lifetime. Revelations 2:17b says that in the end Christians will receive "a white stone with a new name written on it, known only to the one who receives it" (LB). There is power in the name of Jesus to heal and change a person. Let Him give you the promise of a new name now and live in that future.

Chuck Anderson

Printed in the United States
By Bookmasters